From the a

"Poetically Yours, For The Heart Speaks,"

3/24/05

Between

Nonnie:

*The legacy
of us lives on
because of the
major gifts you
have given (our
children) Randy*

*Thank you
Happy B-Day*

Mothers

&

Sons

...A Journey of Healing

By Don E. Miller

Don E. Miller

you@@@hotmail.com

FIRST EDITION

Copyright   2002 by Don E. Miller,

Young, Bold, Unique Publishers

Back Cover picture by Backhaus Photography

Manufactured in the United States of America

ISBN: 0-9710951-9-1

Filed with Library of Congress 2002

Table of Contents

Purpose of the book

Dedication

First, all praise and honor go to my LORD and Savior Jesus Christ for giving me the gift of writing. My heartfelt thanks go to the following persons: my beautiful wife, Victoria, for keeping me focused and loving me unconditionally; thank you also for collaborating and working tirelessly on this book with me; my mother, Bernice Miller, for giving me the drive never to quit; my dad, Walter Miller, who never had a chance to see me grow, but I am grateful that I was his seed; my pastor, Reverend Dr. Cynthia Hale of The Ray of Hope Christian Church in Decatur, GA., for your spiritual guidance and being a "woman of excellence;" Reverend Dr. Trunell Felder, my other pastor, your prayers and words of encouragement helped me to see things from God's perspective. Thanks also to my community fathers– Walter Hawkins, Cleveland Reed, Bob Turner, Ike Jones, and Dick Jacobs. Also to those men that saw talent and encouraged me – Andy Gasparovic, Bob Thomas, Marty Kirsch, Tim Gianonni, Tom Wilt, Bob Parsell, Mike McArdle, Ron Lipscomb and my father-in-law, Alphonse Forrestier. A special thanks goes to Dr. Stephen Wright of Seminole Community College for helping me to develop my writing skills. Thanks also to the National-Louis University, Atlanta staff (Jamie, Shirley, Faye and Dr. Mendoza and others) for your support. Thanks to my Boys & Girls Clubs family for the opportunity to serve. Thanks to Dr. Sharon Tanner for "Standing In The Gap," and to Joyce Ogletree for your editing contribution. Thanks to all the educators that are committed daily to teaching and developing the leaders of tomorrow.

Most importantly of all, thanks go to the men who shared their stories and the mothers who gave them a story to tell. I have not listed your names because you know how your mama is (smile).

Purpose

The purpose of this book is to celebrate the influence that mothers have provided to men. Mothers have provided the nurturing and stability to the lives of most men in America, especially within the Black communities. When fathers were absent from the family, mothers provided the glue that held many families together. In most minority families we have what is called a *matriarchal society* – mother rules. This book will also focus on insights that may be useful to young mothers raising their sons. It will also provide insights to mothers that may need to heal the relationship with their sons. This book will hopefully provide women with clues concerning what men think, how they think, and how men care about women. There is a statement that goes like this, "If you want to know how a man will treat you, observe how he treats his mother." There is a lot of truth in this statement.

This book is not a book to negate the father-son relationship. Being a male, I understand the importance and necessity of having positive male influences in the lives of every young man. We need more males involved in every aspect of young men's lives to help them navigate through issues such as sexuality, education and careers. There is a section in the book that will focus on the role of fathers in the lives of males.

The relationships discussed in this book will inspire, convict, and cause laughter and appreciation of the relationships between mothers and sons. To illustrate the power of the mother-son relationship, I have interviewed ten men who have graciously shared the stories of their relationship with their mothers. They have discussed how their relationships shaped them into the men they are today, and even impacted the women they dated and later married.

Inception

One night my wife and I were in the kitchen talking to one of our nephews. He began making negative comments about how his mother viewed him and how she felt about him. His father and other brother walked in and began sharing their views about their mothers. (These brothers have different mothers). I joined in the discussion sharing similar experiences that I had with my mother. We all discovered that we had two things in common: hurt and acceptance over our mothers' lack of affection towards us.

The next morning as my wife and I were driving to work, my wife brought up the discussion that was held the night before. It was amazing that even though all four of us were different ages, had four different mothers, and four different backgrounds, yet our pain was identical. Our ages ranged from 15 to 45. We each had deep-seated hurt concerning our relationships with our mothers and we were all at different stages of working through our hurt and rejection from our mothers. The conversation opened up wounds and allowed us a chance to focus on the things that would bring us to a point of healing, reconciliation or acceptance of our mothers. This conversation between four very different men was the reason for this book.

Conception

Everything starts with conception. The relationship a mother has with her son starts at conception. This relationship is one of the most significant relationships in a male's life. Mothers and sons have always had a bond. Mothers have always been protective of their sons. We can look back into the history of African Americans. During slavery Black males were usually sold away from their homes, especially the fathers. If the sons were useful (physically strong) they were sometimes separated from the family also. In the absence of the father, the mothers knew it was important to teach their sons about survival. Even though their son's lives were in constant danger because of what they possessed (their physical strength and the desire to be free) mothers still tried to protect their sons.

Today, mothers still have fears concerning their sons' survival. Fear of whether law enforcement will be equitable concerning laws and treatment of Black males. Fear of whether the educational system in America will be equitable concerning resources and programs in teaching and equipping their sons with skills while recognizing and utilizing their abilities regardless of geographical location and home address. Fears concerning whether the corporate structures will be equitable concerning their hiring practices toward their sons' ability to get a job and not be discriminated against because of their racial status. The biggest fear that today's mothers have is that their sons may even be taken out of this world by the hands of another African American male due to the lack of community and the lack of concern we seem to have for each other. The fears that mothers have had increased over the years, and many are even more of a reality in America today.

As we look at America, the number of minorities in prison has increased. Forty-six percent of the prison population is African-American males, yet we make up only 13% of the U. S. population as a race.

Many corporate organizations are having legal actions taken against them (class action suits) due to the mistreatment of minorities. Some educational systems are on the verge of collapsing due to the lack of teachers and resources being placed in minority communities. If children cannot learn, they cannot earn.

Mothers have a bond with their sons because of their love and concern for their welfare. Every mother wants to ensure the possibility that her son will have a better life for himself and his family. If the father did not succeed, the son now has the chance to do it right. If the father was a good father and provider, the son has the ability to take fatherhood to a higher level by being a good provider also. If the father was absent from his children for whatever reason, his son has a chance to be present and available for his children. If the father never finished high school, the son has a chance to achieve a higher standard of education.

Mothers bond with their sons because of the possibilities to fulfill the destiny of a family to be whole. The bond between a mother and son is a foundation for hope and a better tomorrow. It is a bond that is hard to break regardless of the situation and circumstances. It is a bond that needs to be celebrated!

Chapter 1
Stages of Growth

Stages of Growth

This section will cover the various stages of growth that your son will go through. I have outlined each stage along with what mothers need to do and what that stage looks like. Regardless of which stage you may be in with your son, please note that these suggestions are not the only ones that you may need to utilize in your mother-son relationship.

Birth - the initial stage of life through 2 years of age. Things mothers need to be aware of:

- your son will be totally dependant on you
- you will have a separate life again one day
- your love and care are all that your son will remember
- this period is the beginning of the bonding process that everyone must go through in order to feel safe and develop intimacy later in life

What mothers should do:

- take care of yourself
- take care of your son
- pray for your son

- establish a network of supporters, i.e. grandparents, family members, and other mothers with children to help you on this journey of motherhood.
- tell and show your son that you love him
- read to your son daily

Childhood – 2 to 13 years of age. This is the first stage of your son "pulling away". Depending on how well he has learned to bond, the separation stage is usually more painful for the mother than it is for the son, so give your son space to spread his wings. What mothers need to know is that your son:

- still loves you
- wants to be like the big-boys
- will seek to be independent
- still wants your approval, guidance & discipline
- still needs your affection (even if it is in secret)
- still needs you to pray for him
- still wants you to set limits

What mothers should do:

- allow your son more freedom if he has proven to be responsible in the past
- affirm your son every chance you get

- attend as many activities as you can that your son participates in at school or church
- support your son's dreams
- encourage your son to participate in-group activities, i.e. sports, band, etc.
- expose your son to a variety of cultural activities to enlarge his world
- get to know your son's friends
- pray for your son
- tell and show your son that you love him
- read to your son daily
- stress the importance of education, become an active part of the PTA and look over his homework- ask your son about his day at school every day. Ask what he learned each day.

Young Adulthood – ages 14 to 18 years old. This is a difficult stage for young men. This is often the most critical stage of a your son's life. Other males *must* become involved with your son during this stage in order to ensure he is not caught up in the traps that many males get caught up in America (the prison system, gangs, drugs, etc.). During this stage of development your son:

- is not a boy
- is yet not a man

- is in puberty
- has a foot in both worlds (childhood and adulthood)

How it looks:

- his voice changes
- he is more interested in girls and sex
- he will develop a core group of friends
- he now takes an interest in his appearance
- he is talking on the telephone more
- he pulls away from hugs and kisses from mom (shuns affection)

What mothers should do:

- give your son responsibilities at home
- keep structure and expectations
- don't lower you expectations
- discuss sex openly, particularly safe sex
- talk about positive relationships with males/females
- continue spiritual guidance
- make sure his father, uncle or a male mentor is involved and available to your son
- let your son take you on a date so you can teach him how to treat a lady

- pray for your son
- tell and show your son that you love him
- continue to stress the importance of education and remained involved in his education

Manhood – not necessarily an age. This is the age where men are self-supportive. This means they should no longer be living at home with you. What mothers should do:

- cut the apron strings
- be supportive, but not controlling
- let him make his own mistakes and pay the consequences
- do not pick his friends (male or female)
- do not attempt to select his wife
- pray for your son
- tell your son that you love him

Mothers tend to forget that the teaching has already taken place and school is over. "Listen, my son, to your father's instruction and do not forsake your mother's teaching. They will be a garland to grace your head and a chain to adorn your neck." Proverbs 1:8-9 (NIV). You have taught him everything you were able to, but the learning is now up to your son. My father-in-law,

Alphonse Forrestier quotes an old proverb that states, "When the student is ready to learn, the teacher comes." It is now up to your son to be the man that you brought him up to be. Mothers also need to let go and let God continue to walk with your son throughout his life. We are after all, God's sons first, last and always.

Chapter 2

The Role of Fathers

The Role of Fathers
Provider, Protector, Lover

When we examine the relationship between mothers and sons one of the key elements concerning this relationship is the role of the father. Fathers are important in the fiber of development of young males. A father's example teaches young males how to treat, appreciate and respect women of all cultures and backgrounds. Most males grow up in a household where they observe their fathers playing the role of provider, protector and sometimes the lover. Even if the father is in the home or estranged from the family he will still play these roles, even if not consistently. Most of the men that I have interviewed stated that they saw their fathers in the role of provider and protector, but rarely as the lover. Let's examine these roles:

Provider – one who provides financial, spiritual and emotional support to the family. Most men will provide financial support to their families. Working was always something that men did in order for their families to get the support that they needed in order to survive. My father worked as a fruit picker and a foreman to provide for my mother and eight children, yet he did not provide the spiritual and emotional support that we needed. Some of the individuals that I spoke with stated that their father's worked, but they got their spiritual and emotional support from their mothers. Most men have been taught by the examples shown by their fathers, such things as how not to exhibit emotions or tears because it makes a male look weak. Men have the tendency to keep anger and disappointment inside, which causes illnesses such as high blood pressure, ulcers and other physical and emotional problems due to their inability to process anger and disappointments in an appropriate manner.

Protector – one who keeps the security of the family. Again this is a role that most fathers readily fulfill without any resistance. Fathers would make sure that the home was a place of refuge. The home was a place where everyone needed to feel safe. Fathers would not allow the family to be taken advantage of by means of force (breaking and entering, burglary, etc.). The father played the role of the protector to the point that many individuals feared even making an attempt to burglarize or cause the family any unrest. "How can anyone enter a strong man's house and carry off his possession unless he first ties up the strong man? Then he can rob his house." (Matthew 12:29-NIV). Many homes are missing that strong man today.

Lover – the nurturing provider to the mother and the family. Many of the men I interviewed stated that their fathers never told them that they loved them. Their fathers provided the food, clothing and shelter and even provided protection, but their fathers were not able to openly show affection to them and their mothers.

Most men know that a sexual relationship existed between their parents because of the existence of brothers and/or sisters, but they rarely saw a passionate exchange between their parents (affectionate kisses, hand holding, romantic exchanges). Many of the men I interviewed stated that they never saw their dad kiss their mother. Sons should see their fathers in a passionate setting with their mothers and feel comfortable about their parents holding hands and kissing in their presence. The more sons see their fathers in a passionate and appropriate setting with their mothers or their mates, then sons will be more likely to show appropriate passion towards women. The problem is that many sons have seen their fathers in an abusive setting with their mothers. The abuse can range from verbal and emotional abuse to physical abuse (pushing or fighting). Witnessing these behaviors can cause a lot of young men to demonstrate this same type of behavior towards females, which can result in a lack of respect for females. Sons who grow up seeing their fathers showing a lack of respect towards women may result in sons trying to figure out how to treat women or to duplicate their father's behavior.

Fathers also need to show affection towards their sons. One of the men I interviewed stated that the first time his dad told him that he loved him was on his deathbed. This gentleman stated that he knew his father cared because he provided his essential needs, yet his dad did not say the words, "I love you, son," which all males need to hear. As stated earlier, men have problems showing their emotions especially towards each other. Men have been socialized to suppress their emotions except during a major lost (death) or a sporting event.

Sons not knowing that their fathers loved them through words continue to seek their fathers' acceptance throughout their lives. "Not knowing your earthly father has a direct correlation to how men view God as their Heavenly Father," stated Reverend Dr. Cynthia Hale of Ray of Hope Christian Church, in Decatur, Georgia. Men need the support and nurturing of their fathers, which so many times they did not receive.

Fathers do not always need to be biological. Stepfathers sometimes have taken on the role of the biological father to provide support and nurturing to young males. Young males also need other men of influence in their lives in the absence of their biological fathers. This in no way gets the biological fathers off of the hook, but circumstances may arise (death or divorce) that may cause a need for other men to step forward and provide positive influence and support for young males. These surrogate males are what I will call "community fathers." Community fathers can include brothers, uncles, ministers, youth counselors, teachers, and next-door neighbors, etc. These are men who *choose* to have direct involvement in the development of young males whose fathers are absent. My father passed away when I was twelve years old. My first "community father" was my big brother, Clint Blackmon, Sr. While I had a troubled youth, my brother who was in the service at the time, took me to live in Virginia with him and his wife Linda in order to prevent me from going to a Juvenile Detention Home. By taking me in, he prevented me from entering the penal system that many young males find themselves trapped in. My brother's love, caring, and willingness to step up to the plate as a "community father" in place of my father, made all the difference in my world. Clint exposed me to many of the things that I cared about. He knew I loved to dance and that I always wanted to dance on television. Clint took me to the audition of a dance show called, Dance to the Music, which was a syndicated dance show that aired in 55 cities across America. I was able to secure a spot on the television show, thus fulfilling one of my fondest dreams. I thank him for his dedication and belief in me, because without his efforts there would be no telling where I would be today.

Other men from my community that stepped in as "community fathers" include Mr. Lee, Reverend Ivory, Mr.

Thomas Ervin, Sr., Mr. Emmett Jackson, Mr. Johnny, and Mr. David. These were some of the men that taught me to have good work ethics, how to interact with other people and the importance of family. Another male that had a profound impact on my life was Mr. Forest, one of my elementary school teachers. He taught me about self-discipline, how to develop confidence, and what it meant to be prepared for the future.

Men can have a direct or indirect influence on the life of young males. It is vital that men play an appropriate role in the lives of young males. Community fathers have helped shape the lives of many young men in America today.

I remember an incident when I was 15 years old. I was riding the city bus and having a conversation with several other young men my age. I was using a lot of profanity, which was in the presence of women and elderly individuals. The bus driver stopped the bus and came to the back of the bus where I was sitting. He spoke directly to me and said, "Young man, if you want to continue riding on this bus, the language you are using will not be tolerated." I was totally embarrassed and rightfully so. This had such a profound impact on my life—it taught me about respecting women and the elderly. To this day, I am still very respectful and conscious of what I talk about around all females. I often share this story while teaching other young men about the importance of respecting themselves and females. The bus driver, who did not even know me by name, took the time to correct my behavior because he wanted me to be a man of great character. All men must play the role of a community father from time to time. Community fathers are often men that do not desire the spotlight, but prefer to be behind the scenes. They shape the lives of the community and are less talked about for their contributions. Without them our young men and our communities are lost to drugs, crime and violence. The problem often is that we replace the community fathers with other negative types of influences (i. e., drug dealers, gang involvement, anti-social behavior, or sexual involvement), which our young men are being inundated with daily. Most young males are being taught about social issues in the streets by older men and not at home by their fathers. A lot of the information that young men are learning in the community concerning sex, drugs, relationships, etc. is distorted and it can take years to re-program their thought processes.

One of the men I interviewed stated that he learned how to use women at the age of 14 by watching his dad. His father introduced him to older women, which was when he began having sexual relations and letting women spend money on him. Other male friends of his father supported these views. Many young men in America are trapped into this type of thinking due to similar teachings in many communities across the country. This thinking does not only relate to women, but also to spiritual, financial,

A Mama's Boy

In today's society millions of young males are being raised in female-headed households. Regardless of social or economic status, women are still the principle parent when we look at the raising of young men in America. Because of this situation, young men have always been very close to their mothers. "Mama was the one who took care of me when I was sick," or "Mama was the one that talked to me about my disappointments," were comments that were echoed by many of the men interviewed for this book. When you look at major sports figure's speeches of triumph they are always saying "thanks mom" whenever the camera flashed them after scoring a touchdown or some other victory. The relationship between a mother and a son is a very strong bond.

Some women are under the misconception that a "mama's boy" is a man who allows his mother to control his life, love, dreams and ambitions. Some women feel that their roles may be secondary to that of their man's mother and that if the mother does not approve of her son's relationship it is going to be a bumpy and sometimes impossible relationship to maintain. But a "mama's boy" does not necessarily mean that the mother is the controller of her son's life.

When it comes to the type of woman a man chooses to marry, "mama" is usually the model of his ultimate woman.

"When I look at the way my wife moves her mouth in discussions I realize my mama does the same thing," stated another man interviewed for this book. "After dating several women and noticing how they behaved around kids, I could not feel that they would be able to nurture my children like my mother did," stated another man included in this book. Another definition of a "mama's boy" is a man who genuinely loves his mother, and her attributes are important qualities needed or desired in the woman he wants to fall in love with. The first woman who teaches a male about love is his mother, grandmother or whatever female that happens to have been in his life as a child.

Several of the men interviewed in this book spoke about their wives having traits similar to their mothers. Some of the traits were not evident to these men until we had a conversation about the woman they chose to marry. "My mother handled the finances in the home when I was growing up and my wife handles the money now," stated one of the men that I interviewed. "My mother was poor with the finances, so I married someone that was better with money management than my mother," stated several of the men. Even when the mother has negative and positive attributes it will affect the males' view of the females in his life. From cooking to cleaning, nurturing, support or criticism, these are areas where men analyze their relationships in comparison to their mothers. Several of the men stated that they were not consciously looking for a woman that was like their mother when choosing a mate. "I already had a mother so I did not need or want my woman to be like my mother. I now realize after years of marriage that my wife is a lot more like my mother that I first thought," which is what several of the men acknowledged.

A man who genuinely cares for his mother and respects her can really care for his woman. It is hard for a man to love his woman and not love his mother. Unless emotional and or physical abuse has taken place, a man will love his mother in spite of her flaws and disappointments. "I watched alcoholism strip my mother of her beauty, but I still always loved her," stated another man. If a man has a lack of love and respect for his mother, it is certain that he will have a problem maintaining a healthy relationship with a woman. You can discover a lot by examining a man's relationship with his mother. The positive or negative relationship that a son has with his mother should be used as an indicator for women in reference to their relationship with their men.

Women can learn from a mother's mistakes and triumphs. Some men had mothers that were critical so they long for women that are supportive. Some men had mothers that were not nurturing so they long for a woman that is both loving and nurturing. Those men that have or had nurturing mothers will not deal with abusive women. Men who had mothers that were good cooks enjoy a woman who can cook. Learn how to make more than reservations. If you do not know how to cook get a cookbook, take a class, and learn how to cook something. Some mothers have a relationship with their sons where they laugh and talk openly and honestly. A man wants a woman that he can laugh and have fun with and not have to be serious all of the time. If a man can love his mother he can definitely love you.

We know there are men whose mothers control their lives and those men need to learn where their mother's place is. The scripture Matthew 19:5 states: "For this cause shall a man leave his father and mother, and shall cleave to his wife and they shall be one flesh" (NIV).

A woman should not feel threatened by the relationship a son has with his mother, but observe it closely. It could give the woman some clues into the type of man that he is and the type of woman he wants in his life. A woman can also benefit from knowing about the mother-son relationship if she pays close attention to what his mother does and does not do. A woman must still evaluate her relationship with her mate on an individual case basis. The man must love and respect his woman and treat her as God's gift to humanity. But do not forget to check out his relationship with his mother first. This connection will play a vital part in setting the tone for other male/female relationships that every young male will experience in their lifetime. Just as branches are an extension of a tree, men are an extension of their mother. Choose wisely.

Chapter 4
Searching For A Mother's Love

Searching For A Mother's Love

I am a 42-year-old business owner. In spite of all of my accomplishments and endeavors in life I continue to search for my mother's love. From my childhood through my young adulthood I never felt her love was available to me.

My father passed away when I was 12 years old. My parents both were hard workers. While growing up my father was a fruit picker and my mother was a maid. My mother handled the household finances and all the matters concerning the family, ranging from the bills to school and church.

I remember as a child the times when friends of our family came over and I would go into the living room and dance to show off. My mother would smile when I performed, which were some of the happier times at our house. Even though this was a good time in my life, I never really felt a genuine closeness to my mother. I was a very ill child. I suffered from epilepsy. When I was in elementary school I would sometimes have seizures. I do not know if my illness may have played a major role in why my mother felt a certain way about me. She made sure I received the appropriate treatments, hospital visits and the necessary medical care. While these were acts of love, I never heard the words that she loved me. She spent a lot of time coming out to the school due to my misbehaving in class. My father was not active in my life at all, so my mother handled everything. I was always punished for negative behavior. I did not get away with much.

When I attended middle school I joined a singing group. I enjoyed performing and being on stage. My mother never attended any of my performances. I remembered my 8th grade talent show. I was one of the best dancers in the school and had a really good singing voice. I informed my mother that I was going to be in the Soul Train Line and that I would be singing a solo. She did not attend the show, but one of my sisters came and saw me perform. Again, I wanted my mother to be there to see me perform and to feel proud about my accomplishments. I continued to invite my mother to other events where I was performing, yet she never attended any of them. I always wanted to be close to my mother and was always hopeful that I could spend some quality time with her. One day it finally happened.

I entered a contest to win a cruise to Jamaica. I won the contest and took my mother as my guest on the cruise. We laughed and had a good time together. This was the first time that I had my mother all to myself. I was in my late twenties when the cruise took place. This cruise was my time of healing. After the cruise with every phone call or visit she began to tell me that she loved me and that she always did. The trip allowed us to talk about her life and her struggles with me as a child and her own disappointments.

My mother's impact on my life caused me to strive to be the best that I could be. She had very high work ethics. I remembered when my father was ill, my mother and I cleaned office buildings at night and she would return home and then report to her day job. She later got a job working with the county, which she retired from about 10 years ago. I learned how to work for what I wanted. My mother also taught me how to pray. I remembered when the food was low and money was scarce, I would see my mother cry and fall on her knees and pray.

One of the greatest moments in my life with my mother came while at my wedding reception. I had spoken with several of the wedding guests and my wife and I had already completed our first dance. I went over to the table and asked my mother to dance. It had been at least 30 years since I saw my mother dance. My mother and I danced together and it felt like it did when we danced in our old living room.

I finally met and married the love of my life. My wife is a very loving individual. She will not allow me to leave or return home without a kiss and hug. She makes such a fuss over me. It is funny how she carries on because I have never had any woman to love me like she does. I am very appreciative to her for that.

My wife is very resourceful. I often tell the story about her little "drawer." This drawer has *everything* any of us in the house might ever need. Once I told my wife that I needed a light bulb for my Cadillac. My wife said, "go check in that drawer." To my amazement, I found a bulb that fit my car, even though my wife was driving a Tempo at the time. My wife spends a lot of time piddling—meaning she shops for nothing in particular. She can always be found shopping at a discount or department store seeking things that we might need. Her belief is that if the family needs anything it should be found at home.

My wife and I came from very different backgrounds. She was adored as a child and as an adult. She has the capacity to draw people into her world because of her warmth and caring personality. I, on the other hand, had a troubled childhood and did not have that type of love and devotion. I guess that is why she pours a lot of herself into me because of my lack of love as a child and her abundance as a child.

My wife has shown me unconditional love and support throughout our marriage. I remember the time I was told that my services were no longer needed on the job. I called her in disappointment and informed her about the situation. Her response was, "Come on home, I still love you." I was expecting her to say that I had better get another job quickly. Instead she told me that her love for me was not based on what kind of job I worked, but that she loved me for the man that I was and that everything was going to be okay. My self-esteem was very low, but she managed to lift my spirits and continues to build me up on all sides. My wife has a zeal for life and a strong spiritual commitment. She has a laugh second to none and she seeks to enjoy life everyday. She believes that God has given us an abundant life and that we should enjoy it. She is an incurable romantic and since I write poetry we are well matched. She brought to me the love that I wrote about in my poems.

My wife and mother are similar in several ways. They both are great cooks, very independent and very stubborn. Both women are very resourceful and both of them love me.

In spite of what I may have missed as a child, I love my mother and always will. She did the best she could with what she had. I admire her diligence and her contribution to making me the man that I am today. I now believe that my mother always loved me, but at times did not know how to show me. Today we talk at least once or twice a week. After each conversation the final words are, "I love you." Her sacrifices allowed me to live my dreams. Now after every business trip or exciting person I meet, I call my mother to tell her how much I appreciate her efforts so that I can now enjoy these experiences.

Moral Lesson: It is never too late to heal your relationship with your son. Regardless of how old your son is, tell him that you love him and how proud you are of him. This will help both of you to heal and will restore your relationship so that your mother-son relationship can once more be a source of joy to both of you. For no matter what your son has accomplished, he still wants and needs his mother's approval. Celebrate your love for each other!

Chapter 5

A Mother's Cry

"A Mother's Cry"

It is a sad feeling to hear mothers cry. A mother's cry is a sound that is very unfamiliar and one that is filled with pain. Mothers cry daily for the survival of their sons. Seeing past situations with their fathers, brothers and uncles concerning some of the injustices cause a cry deep within the heart of most Black mothers. These injustices are the cause of great concern for their male child. The fear of whether their sons will survive the ills of gangs, drugs, AIDS, unemployment and violent crimes are reasons for this eternal cry. I had an opportunity to interview a mother whose cry was one of pain and agony for a son that was lost. Here is her story.

"My son was a young man who was very involved in school activites at a young age. During his younger years, I did not spend a lot of time with him because I had issues of my own. A bad marriage and drugs were the demons that haunted me. My son would often ask me for love, which I felt I gave him, but later realized that I did not really give him what he needed. His father and I had a violent relationship, which finally ended. His father did not spend time with either of us.

As he began to grow up he changed during his teenage years. His grades and his behavior changed. He got involved in drugs and started hanging with a different group of friends. His dress changed, yet I thought it was only a phase he was going through. He would not do what I said, but rather what he wanted to do. This made our relationship very unstable. I tried to keep him out of relationships with girls, which was unsuccessful. How could I teach him how to have an appropriate relationship with *anyone* when my relationship with his father was based on drugs and violence?

He started staying out late and failing classes. I began to see my son slip into a place that was beyond his or my control and I could not stop his journey. He began to get into trouble with the law, because of theft and other petty crimes. He was given some consequences within the justice system, yet these consequences did not cause him to change his behavior. As my son continued on his journey he got more involved in criminal activities. He also developed a relationship with a young lady that I felt had a bad influence on him. This relationship was a major part in his final downfall.

Three young men robbed a store. My son was one of the three young men. My son had no weapon during this robbery, nor was a gun used in the robbery. My son told this young lady about the robbery and she informed the authorities and testified against him. My 23-year-old son is currently serving 55 years in prison for this crime. His life is now a life behind bars.

I talked to my son recently on one of my visits to prison and our conversation brought a revelation to me. My son told me that during his younger years he felt that I did not love him. I mentioned to him that I often told him during his years growing up that I loved him. He responded, 'Yes you *told* me that you loved me, but you never *showed* me that you loved me.' He stated that he did not find love at home, but rather in the streets with the guys and the young girls that he was involved with sexually. This conversation made me realize that my son needed my love then and that he still needed my love now. When we speak today at the beginning and the end of every conversation I tell him how much I love him. I am crying inside because my son is incarserated, but I pray for his release and well being daily. I have grown as this situation continues to unfold in both of our lives. Today we can talk and laugh whereas in the past we could only argue. If I could give any advice to a mother I would say, "Do not only *tell* your son that you love him, but *show* him." I now know that love is an action verb. Support his dreams, attend whatever activities he participates in, and tell him often that you are proud of him and that you love him. Finally, be available for the good, the ugly or the indifference that will certainly arise in your son's life."

This scenario plays out in America on a daily basis. A crime was committed, but was justice equal? A mother's cry is one for justice. This mother's son did break the law, but was the punishment justified? Was justice equal? No life was lost during the robbery. Only the lives of the young men involved by imprisoning them for an unimaginable number of years.

As we see men being released for crimes that they did not commit, but have been imprisoned for sometimes more than 20 years of their lives, we see that injustices are still taking place today.

An example of why racism and injustice to the Black male is a justified fear was exhibited in an incident that happened to me. Early in 2001, I was traveling on Interstate 75 South in Georgia heading towards Florida. I was going to do a book signing and to pick up my daughter to bring her back to Atlanta to look at some colleges. As I was driving through a small town in Georgia a state trooper stopped me. He asked me where I was going. I informed him that I was an author and that I was scheduled for a book signing that day in Orlando, Florida. He advised me that he stopped me because I was speeding (83 miles in a 70 miles per hour zone). I was driving a rental 2001 SUV. While waiting for the ticket to be written, the officer requested me to get out of the vehicle. He told me to put my hands up and he searched me. He called for backup (4 cars with 2 officers each appeared). He told me to move away from the vehicle so they could search it. I moved away from the vehicle with my hands at my side while all of these officers searched my belongings and the vehicle for drugs or any other illegal items. I stood out on the side of the highway in this small town while others passed by watching my vehicle being searched. Not only was I embarrassed, but also in fear for my life. There I stood a Black man with 8 White officers in a small town having the vehicle and my belongings searched. I stood there in disbelief and praying for my own safety. Thank God nothing happened. The officer finally gave me a ticket and allowed me to leave. I was hurting as I was thinking to myself, I have never used nor sold drugs, I do not drink, I am an author, employed and yet my vehicle was searched because I was a Black male driving a 2001 SUV in a small town. The ticket was only $75, but my pain and humiliation was immeasurable. This is the type of event where many Black men have lost their lives, but I survived. This event helped me to realize that no matter what I may accomplish, there are still some people that will pre-judge me because of the color of my skin and that justice is not equal.

I have spoken to mothers from different geographical and economical backgrounds. Most of these mothers agree that their main fear is the injustice in America towards minority males. The racial profiling and other acts of injustice are real fears in minority mothers raising sons with or without fathers. Death is not necessarily the worst thing that can happen to a young man, but imprisonment can be an equally devastating event.

It is very important that mothers tell their sons that they love them through both words and actions. All boys need hugs and kisses or they may eventually begin to drift away. Even if your son appears not to need or want your affection, he still secretly yearns for the warmth of his mother's touch and care as he continues to find himself. So hug and kiss your son anyway!

Just because your son needs your affection does not mean that he is weak, but that he has a genuine affection and admiration for his mother.

Moral Lesson: Contrary to popular belief, it is not the designer clothes that are purchased or the things that are given to your son that will have a lasting impact on his life. Your love and presence are the most priceless things you can give to your son. And should tragedy happen to your son, always be his mother and still affirm him through both words and actions.

Chapter 6

The Educator

The Educator

I am in my mid-thirties, never married and am raising my son. I work in the field of education. My mother is deceased.

My parents were affectionate towards each other, but not openly in front of the children. We never saw them kiss or touch each other except maybe holding hands after church. But with nine children, there certainly must have been some affection between them.

My dad handled my disappointments with a "hands-off" approach. My dad's take was that all disappointments led to lessons that helped us learn and grow into better human beings. My mother, on the other hand, was just the opposite. She tried to shelter me from everything or at least offer me comfort.

My mother was neat and orderly and a very good cook. My dad was the provider of the money for the family. My mother was the authority figure – over the kids and my dad. The qualities that I liked about my mother included:

1. Her willingness to give. Ultimately she put her family first and no sacrifice was too great for the good of the family. She even quit her job to help me raise my son.

2. Her strength and endurance throughout her lifetime.

3. Her refusal to let others define who she was.

4. She always offered encouragement to all of her children.

5. She did not want anything for herself.

The quality I disliked about my mother was her pride, often to the point of her detriment. An example of this was if she asked one of us to do something and if we did not do it within a certain timeframe (what she deemed reasonable), she would do it herself. Like the time she asked us to mow the lawn. Because we did not do it within the timeframe she felt it should have been completed, she went outside and mowed the lawn herself.

Her personality type was mostly aggressive. She did not have a lot of education, but she pushed all of her children to get a college degree because she believed that education was the key to success for us in America. As a result of my mom's desire for us to be well educated, I not only graduated from college, but I continued going to school until I earned a PHD in education. I took a sabbatical from the school system and took my son with me to a different city in order to complete this degree. My mother's directive to each of us was that we should define ourselves and never let society or anyone else define us.

She was very active in each of our schools. Everyone at our schools knew who she was and that she would come to the school for any and everything. She was a very active parent. Her decision-making skills were spontaneous. She spent from her heart, and she spent everything. Often when my dad said no she still managed to get her way and she bought what she felt her family needed. Like the time my big brother was going to a prom and the car had bald tires. My dad was willing to take a chance that his son would return home safely, but my mom would not have it. She got the credit card and went out and purchased four new tires for the car. My brother did arrive home safely from the prom.

An open display of affection towards her children was rare. My mom did not openly give her children hugs and kisses. She showed us how much she cared for us by the things she did for us. I was the only one of her children that she kissed.

Most of the women I dated were more affectionate than my mom. Like my mom, these women were also very good with finances. As for support, I am not open to letting many women into my personal issues and concerns. While I have dated mostly passive women in the past I prefer to date aggressive women because I believe there is strength in aggression. I would like to feel that if something happened to me that my wife would be able to carry on in my absence.

The qualities that I am seeking in a wife include:

1. An educated woman (college) or at least seeking to get to another level in her personal growth.

Chapter 7

The Ultimate Father

The Ultimate Father

I am in my early forties, work in the education system, and married with three children. The affection I saw between my mother and father was plentiful. I saw lots of hugs, kisses on the neck and other forms of affection between my parents. My father was the breadwinner and my mother was a housewife.

My mother was very clean. In fact we always jokingly referred to her as a "cleaning machine." My mom was also a great cook. In our home my father was the ultimate disciplinarian, but while dad was at work my mom did not hesitate to step in and do her part. My mom both spanked and yelled at us. But that was by no means the end—"wait until your daddy gets home for the rest." With my father, the sight of his belt brought tears to our eyes.

The qualities that I liked most in my mother included her unselfishness; she did anything to ensure the basic needs of our family were met. She actually sacrificed her goals and dreams for her kids. She never finished high school, because she got married, and then the kids started coming. She always dreamed of becoming a writer, but circumstances did not allow her time. My daddy wanted her to be a housewife, so that is what she became. The quality I disliked about my mom was her ability to get mad--- she had a keen, screeching voice---it was like God's wrath coming down when she got angry.

I saw my mom as an assertive woman. She was often soft spoken and quiet. Even though she was small in size, she was large in statute and she had a big presence. Her decision-making skills were well thought out. She always discussed everything with my dad and the family if necessary. My dad always supported whatever decision my mother made.

To my mom education was vital, not an issue to be compromised or discussed. Each of her children was going to finish high school and even attend college. As for dating, my mom did not think I was ready to start dating. Even though I am married, my mom never thought that I was ready. She felt like I was so carefree that dating would be a hindrance to me completing my education. She believed that all young men must learn responsibility before they should settle down. My mom was very good with money. She was very resourceful. She grew her own food in a garden and even made our families' clothes. The only things we really shopped for were shoes. My mom was very affectionate with my siblings and me. She recited poetry, gave us lots of hugs and kisses. She demonstrated her love and affection through cuddling and open affection. While she did not spare the spankings, she always wanted to talk about whatever problem that was causing me pain.

In spite of her affection, my mother was often very critical when it was something she did not understand. Like when I wanted to play football in school, my mom was totally against it. On the other hand if it was something for my good, she was always very supportive. My determination helped my mom realize that I was able to accept whatever responsibility went along with my decisions.

I have been married to the same woman for over ten years. My wife, like my mother, is very affectionate. She will reach for my hand anyplace we are together. I think this is rare because you do not frequently see an open display of affection between Black males and females these days. Like my mother, my wife helps me to handle my disappointments.

The qualities I like about my wife include that, like my mother, she is very giving to anyone in need. She will even volunteer my services if the need arises. She loves God and our children. But the main quality that I love about my wife is that she cares about my well-being. Some similarities between my wife and mother are that both women are very resourceful, both are seamstresses, both love kids, both love God and both women are very caring.

At first I did not choose my wife because of any similarities to my mother. Honestly, I wanted someone totally different than my mom because I did not want another mother, I already had one. I knew I did not want a woman that smoked, drank or was a party animal. I wanted a homemaker, like my mom. One thing that attracted me to my wife was that she was not afraid to come into my world. She was willing to learn about jazz, football and basketball. In exchange, she took me into her world. I had to learn how to share her interests also. Now, over the years I have learned to have a genuine interest in the same things that interest my wife.

Since my mother made our house a home when I was growing up, I knew that I wanted to be a father and to raise a family. Our family cleans the house as a project so that my wife does not the have full responsibility for the upkeep of the house since she works outside of the home.

The special qualities that my mom possessed included being a "life-teacher." My mom instilled a lot of information about getting an education, self-respect, and how to be self-disciplined. She also taught me that I should always leave a positive impression on others.

The one quality that I wish I could have changed about my mother was her ability to be overly critical. She often thought the whole world was out to get you, she practiced old superstitions, and often told tales of doom and gloom. Along with this, she often compared me to others. It often hurt my self-esteem to be compared to others, especially when I did not measure up to them in my mom's eyes. My dad tried to compensate for her criticism by telling me how special I was.

My mom had such a profound effect on me because she was the first woman in my life. She was the centerpiece of our home, she was the preacher, the doctor, and she ran the show. Mom solved problems, my mom's hand rubbed me down, and she kissed whatever hurt me and made it feel good, even if I thought I was going to die.

Outside of my wife, my mom is my best friend. My mom and I reached this point because I initiated a discussion about my childhood experiences. I told my mom how I felt growing up because I chose to be healed. Her response was, "I only wanted to make you into the man that God wanted you to be."

My sister taught me that it was important to respect any woman that I cared about. She also taught me what a woman looked for in a man. My sister explained that a man thinks he pulls a woman, but the woman really pulls him! My sister taught me to pay attention to the signs, to watch how a woman dresses, not for herself, but for others. A woman will look a certain way in order to attract a certain type of man.

After I graduated from high school my father passed away, just before I was to leave for college. This was a very painful time in my life. The planning of the funeral was very emotional for the whole family. At the funeral parlor, the director asked my mom who she preferred to walk her down the isle during the ceremony. She answered, "My baby." She did not want my older brother or my baby sister, but *me.* That moment turned our entire relationship around. The fact that she chose me did something to my heart. In spite of all the whippings and criticism she had given me during my life, I knew in that instant that I was loved and that I meant something to her. Well, I stood 20 feet tall, grabbed my mama's hand and I proceeded to walk down the aisle with a sense of pride. God – I felt like daddy. You see my daddy *always* walked with my mom and I was "taking his place." By her choosing me, she told me in so many words that I was now a man.

When I left for college later that summer with no friends or family, everyone thought I left with nothing. But I had my mama and my daddy with me in my heart. When I walked on that campus I knew I was not going to leave that school without my degree. By doing what she did, my mom gave me a purpose. I knew from then on that I wanted to be a man like my daddy. My wife and I adopted three children that I love because they afford me the opportunity to be a father like my daddy. As a result of her never-ending love and faith in me, my mom helped me to become the man and the father that I am today.

Author's Note: This man has achieved a master's degree in special education. He is a teacher and has a business where he counsels trouble children. The relationship he had with his mother and his childhood planted the seeds of him wanting to be a father to many children. He has accomplished this goal through the adoption of his three children and his life's work helping children in crisis.

Moral Lesson: By creating a loving and stable environment for your family, you are helping your son desire to also become a good father. Once the healing has taken place within your mother-son relationship, your son will be able to enter into his role as a father and husband with confidence and devotion.

Chapter 8

The Entrepreneur

The Entrepreneur

I am in my early forties, married to the same woman for almost twenty years and have two children. Overall, I rate my relationship with my mother as being the major factor in contributing to my being the man that I am today. I am the owner of a janitorial business that is very successful.

Growing up I did not see affection exchanged between my parents. My parents were not married to each other, but they lived about a mile apart. In spite of this fact, both of my parents spent time with me throughout my entire childhood.

My parents had a mysterious relationship. They were not loving to each other, but close throughout the week. Because of drugs and alcohol use, their demons came out on weekends through fighting and the attempted stabbing of each other. My years between 8-17 were spent keeping both of my parents alive.

My mother was the only parent that dealt with my disappointments. Since I saw my mother as a strict disciplinarian I rarely had disappointments or problems for her to deal with.

My mother was neat and orderly and she was a great cook. My mother provided the financial support to our family. My mother was a migrant worker in a small town in Georgia and did not make much money. To the best of my knowledge, I did not see my dad contribute financially to our household.

As for affection my mother provided all of the affection I knew as a child. She kissed and praised me often throughout my childhood. My dad on the other hand did not show any affection in the same way. Although I often saw my dad in the presence of his female friends, he never showed me how to treat women. He would pick me up on Fridays and for the entire weekend he would drink at his female friends' houses. Often he was so drunk that I would have to drive us home. As a result of these episodes I learned how to drive at 11 years old. My father was irresponsible.

The only quality I disliked about my mother was her drinking habit. Even though she was a large woman, she was very beautiful. She had excellent bone and facial structure that alcohol use destroyed, but she always remained beautiful to me.

The qualities I liked most about my mom included her ability to show lots of love to everyone, her openness to giving affection and her ability to give to anyone who had a need. I saw my mother share her $10 a week check with her sister in order to help her sister support her 6 kids. Now, that's love!

As for my mother's personality trait, she was passive aggressive. She often worked two jobs just to make ends meet. Even though she was able to manage money well she often demonstrated a Jekyll & Hyde personality. During the week she was the perfect person (Jekyll). But from Friday to Sunday nights she drank (Hyde). I never understood how she was able to cut it off cold on Sunday nights. Then on Monday mornings the cycle started all over again.

My mother's decision-making skills were spontaneous at best. Often my mom could not afford the things I desired, but somehow she always managed to give me what I wanted. Like the time I wanted a pair of Chuck Taylor tennis. Mysteriously, a few days later I received the tennis. I never really knew how things happened, just that they did.

Another time I wanted a television set. My mom purchased the set and told me that it was mine, just mine. It was a strange thing that while I was growing up I never knew that I was poor until I went away to the service. My mom made me feel rich and special throughout her entire life.

My mom provided me with affection and encouragement at all times. She attended every event that I participated in even though she did not have a car, nor did she know how to drive. As a child my mother taught me to be very respectful, I had to speak to everyone. My mom taught me that it does not cost you anything to be courteous and respectful. Today I still wave at folks on the street because I remember what my mom taught me.

My mom was also very particular about the girls I went out with. We often talked about fast and easy girls. My mom told me to stay away from these females. The other traits that my mom instilled in me included always having self-respect, sharing whatever I have, and to always give generously.

I met my wife when I was 18 years of age while in the service. My wife, like my mother, is very good with finances. She makes sure everyone gets paid. I, on the other hand, want to save all of the money. Together my wife and I have achieved a financial balance within our household. My wife is very caring and giving just like my mother.

I think the key to being close with your mate is constant communication. My wife, like my mother provides a lot of encouragement, especially with my business. My wife is also very neat and orderly like my mother. She is very particular about everything being in its proper place. At first my wife was not a very good cook. I remember when we first met she cooked the worst Thanksgiving dinner I ever had to eat. But I ate it and gave her encouragement. Over the years, she has improved to the point that her cooking can now be compared positively with my mom's cooking skills.

When dating my wife, I was not consciously aware of any connection between these two women. Not until they met each other and had an instant connection that I saw how similar these two women were. At their first meeting it became apparent why I liked my future wife more than any other woman I had previously dated. My wife's maturity level was a lot like my mom's. My wife is also very resourceful. As a matter of fact, I believe that I would not be where I am today if it had not been for my wife and what she has brought into my life. When I started my business my wife told me that I was the visionary and that I had a great business sense. That statement meant a lot to me because I value what she thinks.

I am openly affectionate towards my wife especially in front of my children. Often they will say things like, "Cut that out, or get a room." I know they say these things in fun, but I want them to know how a woman should be treated. Every opportunity I get to be around my wife, I take it because I want to be close to her. I want my children to see me love my wife, so they in turn will learn how to love their wives. My oldest son has a girlfriend that looks just like his mom. I believe the "family root" runs deep and must be protected at all times and at all costs.

The advice I would give to other men concerning their wife/lady and children is to show them as much affection as possible. Fake it in front of the kids if you have to. Otherwise you may end up raising a kid that may spend time in prison because today's women will not tolerate too much foolishness. Teach your sons what it means to respect all women. They watch the example you set by how you treat their mother.

There was never a rift or breakdown in my relationship with my mom. We always remained close. Even on the night of her death I knew it even before the phone rang. I felt her presence in the room so strongly that it frightened me. Twenty seconds after I felt the force, the phone rang and I was told that my mother has just passed away. I always felt close to my mom until the day she died.

My relationship with my mom was so good that I ultimately married a girl just like my mom. A woman who never gives up on me, always loves me no matter what comes, and never allows me to give up on myself. In essence, my wife picked up where my mom left off.

Author's Note: In spite of his very poor beginnings while growing up in a small, rural town, this man graduated from college, is happily married with children and has a very lucrative janitorial business. So no matter how he began, with his mother's love and teachings he grew up to be a man that his mother would certainly have been proud of.

Moral Lesson: The love, care and encouragement that you give your son today will remain with him throughout his life. Even if you are financially poor, the love you give to your son will always make him feel rich. Your son will some day appreciate everything that you have done for him, so continue to give him your best.

Chapter 9

Grandma's Hands

"Grandma's Hands"

I am 36 years, and married with two children. I am currently employed as an editor with a business publishing company. "My mother and father were very affectionate towards each other. My mother and father would kiss sometimes in my presence. My mother passed away when I was twelve years old.

During my younger years my mother was always supportive of the things I wanted to do. Both of my parents worked. My father was a pharmacist and my mother was a teacher. I grew up in a very stable home from what I viewed back then, at least what I thought was stable by having both parents living in the same household. We had money from my birth through 16 years of age. I did not experience a lack of anything. My mother usually had up to eight months of her paychecks in the bank. During this time my father made enough money so that she did not have to spend any of her money.

My mother was the disciplinarian, but my father was there to support her if I got out of hand. My mother was very competent and very encouraging to me. She always kept me reaching for more. Even though I felt my mother was encouraging me, I always sensed she was depressed at times. Depressed because of the treatment she received from my father.

Once my mother passed away I really had no true way of knowing how to treat women. My father and grandfather did more things to damage my understanding of how to treat women than they did to help me. I learned negative behavior from the way I saw both of them treat women. I started dating girls and having sex when I was only 14 years old because my father introduced me to them. He taught me how to hustle and never let anything get you down. He also taught me how to get over on people. My grandfather's only focus was to teach me how to get money. His motto was "Cash is king," meaning once you get money it would solve all of your problems. He was so tight with money that he would squeeze the eagle off of a dollar bill. My father was later incarcerated for drug dealing. That left me only with my mother's social security as a means for my financial support. My father and grandfather did not get along because my grandfather was still angry over my mother's death. My grandmother finally stepped in and took over. My grandmother continued to raise me as a Catholic up to the age of 27. She would always give me prayers. She always watched Oral Roberts on television and she taught me a lot about faith and how to pray about situations. She made me read prayers from a book called _Life Study Fellowship._ She advised me to read and memorize certain prayers for a two-week period so that I would be familiar with them and learn how to utilize them in any given situation. She was not a very educated woman, but she always believed in prayers.

During my sophomore year in college I was going through some prayers my grandmother had given me. Although I was living the "wild college life," I knew that I needed to pray, which is what I did. One day I stumbled across a prayer that said, "Lord help me to find someone nice to love." I laughed at first when I read the prayer. I wondered why she had included this one in my stack of prayers. I found myself praying this prayer through the end of the semester. By the end of the summer of my sophomore year I met my future wife. We began to talk as if we knew each other for a long time. When I returned home with my new wife, many people stated that my wife reminded them of my mother. Her hair, her smile and her personality were very similar. My wife was not what I had earlier visualized as the woman of my dreams, but she was the woman God had for me. She has the competency and the encouraging qualities just like my mother.

Grandma knew something that I later learned, that prayer changes things. Grandma's teaching me the importance of prayer early on in my life not only impacted my life as a young man, but also influenced my daily practice of prayer in my life today.

Author's Note: This man graduated from college and has a degree in law. As a result of his grandma's teaching he has a very strong spiritual life and has a leadership role at his church.

Moral Lesson: Teach your son about the power of prayer and even if he departs from it, he will eventually return to it. Grandmas' hands, like mothers' hands are still sweet and powerful.

Chapter 10

Keeping Me Steady

Keeping Me Steady

I am a 36-year-old graphic artist. I have never been married, nor do I have any children. As I look back over my life I realize what a major role my mother played. My mother had three sons and I am the youngest. She gave birth to me in her mid 40's. By that time, all of the spankings and punishment for children was out of her system, or so I thought.

I remember one afternoon when I was standing on the corner with some of my friends. My mother always called out my name in the neighborhood when she wanted me to come home. She called and I ignored her. I told my friends that I was not going to leave because I was not ready to go home yet. As I continued to stand there with my friends engaged in a conversation, the group of guys I was with began to spread apart. It was like Moses stretching his staff across the Red Sea. No message or verbal clues were given to me, so I kept talking. Little did I know that my mother was walking down the street to see why I did not respond to her call. She proceeded to take charge of the situation, which was to be more than a verbal lashing. I was about 16 years old and I have never forgotten that beating. To this day, whenever my mama calls I respond appropriately and quickly.

Both my mother and father worked. My father was a carriage driver for tourists that visited the French Quarters in New Orleans. My mother was a press operator at a cleaner. I never saw a lot of affection between my parents during my childhood or adulthood. My mother handled all of the issues within the house and anything concerning me. Whenever I had a problem in school or in relationships when I got older, my mother's ear and heart were always with me. My father was not active in my life. As a matter of fact, the first and only time my father ever told me that he loved me was on his deathbed.

When I had any disappointments my mother always had a positive response. When I was younger I always liked to sing and took my singing very seriously. As a teenager I once entered a talent show where I did not perform up to my own expectations. As a result I did not win and was very hurt and disappointed. I talked to my mother about the event and she told me, "Son, there will be times when you will be disappointed, but don't give up. Always keep trying." The advice I received that day has impacted me throughout the rest of my life and I apply those words to my daily life.

My mother still continues to this day to encourage me in any endeavor I undertake. She still shares her wisdom and her personal struggles as a way to let me know that I can make it. My mother always did and continues to show her love both verbally and physically to me.

Currently I am still single by choice. As a result of how my mother raised me, I just want the simple things in life. I want a nice meal, good conversation and a time for solitude. I would like to have a woman that can cook, but if cooking is not her strong suit, that too would be okay because my mother taught me how to cook. But I am looking for a "New Orleans" type woman. That is, a woman that enjoys having fun, honest and open in her conversation, family oriented and who does not play a lot of games. And finally, I need a woman who loves God. For the most important thing that my mother taught me was that a woman who loves God will be able to love my future offspring and me. The love and support that my mother gave me kept me steady on the course of not using drugs, staying away from gangs and generally to be a law-abiding citizen. Because of her love and devotion to me I always wanted to be a son that she could be proud of. Her love also keeps me steady on my course to seek the woman of my dreams and not to marry just anyone.

Moral Lesson: Mothers should continue to pour themselves into their sons by being supportive and loving. By giving your son the best of yourself, you are the model that he will use when seeking a mate.

He will also strive to live up to your expectations of him, so set expectations!

Chapter 11

The Master's Hand

The Master's Hand

I am a minister and in my early forties. I recently married for the first time. Growing up I was very close to my mother. There is an 8-year difference between my mother's last child and me. I was her baby and spent a lot of time with her. My dad traveled a lot on business and my brothers and sister had their own lives since they were older than I was. Nobody wanted to be bothered with a little brother much younger than they were, so I spent even more time with my mother.

My parents were very affectionate towards each other. I saw my dad hug, kiss and play a lot with my mom when he was home. My dad was so smooth. He always managed to make my mother smile. He was always bringing her flowers and gifts, he was quite the Casanova. Watching them, I learned early what love was supposed to look like between a husband and his wife. Because I was so close to my mother I also saw how my dad's negative behavior affected my mother, which taught me the importance of always being sensitive and protective of a woman's heart. My brothers actually taught me about women and how to be "a nice dog." My mother on the other hand always taught me to "treat folks like you want to be treated."

My dad was the disciplinarian of the family. He always tried to listen to my point of view whenever I had a problem. My mother on the other hand would encourage me by saying, "Baby, when you've done your best, you can't do any more." Both of my parents were very supportive. My dad was the breadwinner of the house, but my mom was the accountant and she could handle and count money without a calculator. She always kept everything going.

My mother was a balance of aggression and passivity. She did not like to fight, but she knew how and when to stand her ground. She always loved everyone and she was very just in her treatment to all people. I believe mama's come with a special label. My mother was very affectionate, encouraging, and a great planner. She always had a way of offering only constructive criticism. She was never afraid to let me know how to be better whenever I missed the mark. She was an excellent cook. The only thing I did not like about her was when she fussed. She would go on and on and on. The one thing I wish I could have done for my mother was to encourage her to run after her own dreams. She gave up some of her dreams so her husband and kids could achieve their goals. My mother was matriarch-focal, meaning she was very strong and kept the family together. She did not voice her opinion unless solicited, nor did she tell us what to do. The best quality about her was that she did not smother me.

While dating, I always liked women that were smarter than myself. Even though my mother did not pursue a career outside of the home, I loved sharp, career-oriented women. Unfortunately, most of the sharp women I dated did not have the compassion that I was seeking for my offspring. While dating, I sub-consciously speculated if my children could suckle from this woman's breast and what would they be able to glean from her. Unless they were smart and possessed the same qualities as my mother, all of them lost out, until I met my wife.

My wife and my mother are very similar. They both love family, both are very clean, have the ability to encourage and support my dreams and most importantly, they both love the LORD. My mother was the model and my wife was the perfect match. She possessed all of the traits and characteristics that I wanted in a wife. I am truly blessed to have her as my life's partner.

The other woman that affected and influenced me deeply was my grandmother. My grandmother was a real jazzy lady. She married four times, the last time at 80 years of age. She raised five kids alone, which was quite an accomplishment during her era. She too was a very prominent figure in my development. She taught me to respect women of all ages and also how to value their contributions.

As a result of having these women in my life, I have learned how to be sensitive to all women and how to encourage women to be all that they can be. Having been surrounded by strong women all of my life, they have taught me how to be around other strong women without feeling intimidated and how to be the man that God created me to be.

Author's Note: As a result of his mother's encouragement, love and devotion, he has a PHD in religion, and has gone on to be a minister of the Gospel, leading a congregation of 4000+ members. He is highly respected and esteemed within the church community.

Moral Lesson: Be supportive of your son's dream. Make sure not to smother him. Your son has a natural tendency to be sensitive to your needs. Continue to teach him the importance of how to treat women and how to serve God. These lessons will make a difference in his life.

Chapter 12

The Writer

The Writer

I am a 31-year-old writer. I am married and have no children at this time. I was previously employed as an engineer, but decided a year ago to follow my passion, which was writing.

My mother and I had a close relationship. Even though she did not tell me that she loved me, she always showed me that she loved me. When I think back to my childhood, I remember fondly that my mother used to put my head in her lap while she rubbed my head. This was very comforting to me. Around my house neither of my parents used a lot of words. My mother was more of an action person.

My parents were never openly affectionate in front of me. I only remember seeing them kiss twice while growing up. I used to sneak into their bedroom at night to watch television. One night my mother made a romantic advance to my father and he began snoring very loudly. That was her clue that nothing was going to happen that night. I learned the things that made females happy by watching television because I did not think that my parents knew how to be creative when it came to romance. My mother was aggressive and my father was passive. I remember my mother used to argue with my dad because he often failed to respond to her. They sometimes had heated arguments due to the differences in their personalities.

At home my mother was the disciplinarian. She did not spoil me or let me get away with anything. Her aggressive style was utilized throughout my childhood and teen years. I remember once when I did something that warranted a whipping, my parents threatened to beat me. I told my mother, "The 4-H lady told me that you are not supposed to be whipping me anymore." Well, you can image the whipping I got as a result of that comment. Then my father took over and continued the whipping. After that, I forgot what the 4-H lady said and never mentioned her again.

My mother did not mince words and she was sometimes critical of me. I remember a time in high school when I studied long and hard for a chemistry test. When I made a "D" on the test, I was disappointed and talked to my mother about the grade. Her response was, "It's ridiculous that you made a "D" on that test, but when you turn 18 you can move out of the house because you are not going to graduate from high school anyway." I was very hurt by her comment, but the event did not end there. The next day I had a doctor's appointment. Upon returning home my mother wanted to know how the visit went. Because I was still hurt and angry over her previous comment, I refused to talk to her about the visit. She stood in front of me and continued asking me questions even though she realized I did not want to talk to her. So finally I said, "The doctor told me that when I turn 18 I could move out because I was not going to graduate from high school anyway!"

At that point my mother tried to slap me, but I managed to block the blow. I told her, "You're my mama, if I can't come to you, then I can't go to anyone." I then left to live with my grandmother for the next two days. I returned home, and to this day, my mother and I have never had this type of incident again.

One area where my mother always supported me was in the area of sports. While in school, anytime I did not perform up to my own expectations my mother would always tell me just to stay focused. This meant a lot to me and as a result, I was very successful in sports.

My mother also managed the household finances. Both of my parents worked, my mother was a supervisor with the government and my father was a truck driver. My mother achieved a college degree in journalism and my dad achieved his high school diploma.

I met my wife while in college. One thing I love about my wife is that she is very loving. We say, "I love you" at least ten times a day to each other as a constant reminder of what we mean to each other. These words help me to feel my wife's passion for me. Her constant display of affection motivates and brings me fulfillment, which is what sustains our marriage. My wife was the most passionate woman I ever dated. Her sultry voice really turned me on. My wife is very different than my mother. My wife is assertive, unlike my mother who is aggressive. My mother managed the finances while I grew up, but I mange the finances at my house. My wife is a super counselor and is very compassionate to those around her. Whenever I am disappointed by anything my wife manages to help me re-think my goals and to keep them realistic. She is never critical. My wife is also an excellent cook. As a result of her cooking ability, I no longer have to spend time at McDonalds, Burger King and other fast food restaurants like I did when I was younger. (You know what I mean).

The two things that my wife and mother have in common is that both of them belong to the Delta Sorority and that they both love me.

The main thing I love about my mother is her commitment to family. While in high school I was going through our family album. I saw their wedding picture and noticed a picture of me next to them. I was puzzled so I asked, "Was I there?" I turned the picture over and saw that their wedding picture was dated 1972, and my picture was dated 1970. So in my mind I realized that I was an unplanned pregnancy. I admire the fact that my parents chose to get married *after* I was born, and that they are still married today. I admire that in spite of the fact that they did not have a good marriage, my mother still had another child and remained committed to what she started. I do not think that if I had been in this same situation that I would have had the ability to stick to it.

The other quality I like about my mother was the discipline she gave out. I did not like it then, but because of it I now have respect for the law and those in authority.

The one thing that I wish I could change about my mother is her "generational pride." My mother always has been secretive about issues regarding her family, i.e. finances, children, etc. I wish she was more open and was able to disclose information about these subjects.

Today, my mother and I have a good relationship. When she calls we talk about life and the things that I am doing. She and my wife have a very good relationship. As a matter of fact, my mother talks more to my wife than to me. I have both a wife and a mother that I love, and I am living my dream, therefore I am blessed.

Moral Lesson: Through your life your son will learn the importance of commitment. Also, by giving him discipline you will be teaching him why and how to respect authority.

Chapter 13

Women Men Date or Marry

Women Men Date or Marry

Whether you are a mother reading this book or the woman dating or married to a man whose mother is still alive, here are some tips to help you create a positive atmosphere by which your relationship can flourish.

- *Never* refer to your male's mother negatively. It is okay for him to talk about her, but not you (just listen).
- Be supportive of his dreams and listen to his fears (this creates intimacy).
- Don't be too critical; offer suggestions that will increase his focus towards his goals.
- Don't compromise respect for anything just to have a man (domestic violence, name calling, stereotyping women).
- Keep laughter in the relationship. Do fun things together.
- Learn about his likes and dislikes.
- Develop common interests (movies, sports, dancing).
- Find out about his spiritual life. Does he believe in God, does he attend church *regularly?*
- Find out about his relationship with his mother. Watch how he treats his mother; see how he interacts with her.

Is he respectful, is he harsh or impatient with her; does he argue with her? These are indicators as to how he will eventually treat you.

- Remember that men *usually tend to marry a girl just like their mother*. Learn what are/were the things he loved about his mother and focus on those traits in your relationship. For example, if his mother was a great cook, learn to cook a few good meals. If his mother was a wonderful housekeeper, keep your home orderly. If his mother was concerned about her personal appearance, make sure you focus on how you look. While your man is not looking for you to be his mother, he was attracted to you because of the similarities *between you and his mother*.

- Try to get along with his mother (as much as it is up to you, follow peace with all people). Both you and his mother love this man, so try to get along with her, at least for his sake. I am not advocating becoming a doormat for his mother, but at least behave in a civil manner.

Armed with this information you will be able to improve your relationship with some mother's son.

Chapter 14

Standing in The Gap

Standing in the Gap

While mothers are a vital part of the development of young males, there is still another female that sometimes plays the role of mother. Sometimes in the absence of the mother another female steps up, that is the female teacher.

At least 75 – 80% of all teachers involved in your son's education are female. As women continue to enter the work force, there will continue to be a large percentage of female teachers and administrators that will interact with your son within the school system. Here is a story from a 30-year old man who told me how one of his teachers impacted his life by "standing in the gap" for him.

"I was a young man that had a lot of disciplinary problems while growing up. I would always fight and stayed in trouble. I had both parents in the home, but we were very poor. I also had epilepsy and later had to have an operation that would place a plate in my head.

One day when I was in the sixth grade I was fighting in school. I was beating up this boy and pounding his head into the concrete sidewalk. The kid's head was bleeding badly when a teacher tried to get me to stop fighting, but it took awhile for me to get under control. After this incident my teacher began to take more of an interest in me. She talked to me about my behavior and how I was progressing in school. Up to that point in my life, no one had ever taken an interest in me because of my disruptive behavior. This teacher always told me that I had the potential to be a better person than I was showing everyone.

I went on to graduate from high school and my teacher was very proud of me. Today I am a painter with the same school system that I was terrorizing as a child. Recently, I sent this teacher a dozen of roses as a way of saying "thank you" for believing in me. Because of her interest and belief in me I am a productive citizen today." This is an example of how a teacher was standing in the gap for a family that needed additional support.

I know of another teacher that still takes an interest in her students, even after they have graduated from school. She works with students that have mental and physical limitations and often these children overwhelm their parents. But she remains steady to her course. She takes them to movies, out to eat dinner, and calls to talk to them regularly. These young people are now working and enjoying life due to her commitment to seeing them develop into productive individuals.

In spite of all of the issues of low achievement scores, budget cutbacks and other controversies that sometimes surround our educational system, teachers are daily standing in the gap for parents. A teacher has impacted every doctor, lawyer, sports icon, and Wall Street tycoon. Chances are, that special teacher was a female.

Moral Lesson: Through the support of teachers, young men can be given direction and guidance. A little attention can go a long way towards helping persons achieve their goals. Never under estimate the power of a teacher.

Chapter 15

Conclusion

Conclusion

The mother-son relationship is truly a journey to be celebrated. This relationship sets the tone as how men treat the other women that enter their lives with either honor or disrespect. Most mothers are intentional about how they raise their sons. They may be raising him out of their own fears and disappointments, or even a hope for success where there may have been previous failures. Most mothers want their sons to have a good job, good homes, smart children and a good wife. All of these things society measures as being "the right stuff." Most mothers I have spoken to want their sons to be men of good character and morals, spiritual leaders in the home and in the community.

Often mothers are aware of the things that will cause their sons to have a secondary lifestyle or what some mothers consider, "settling for less than you deserve." That is why mothers make sacrifices such as taking a low-paying job versus a no-paying job or welfare to ensure her son succeeds. That is why if the man leaves the home, instead of giving up, and turning to other methods of comfort, many mothers fall on their knees and cry out to God for an answer. These experiences help their sons learn how to lean and to depend upon God during hard times. This will also help your son develop a prayer life. The reason mothers caught the bus and wore cheaper clothes was so that her son could wear fine linen today. Even when the mother had no education, she worked multiple jobs to ensure that her son could get a higher education. Several of the men stated that their mothers kept things together. This is how many households were able to survive, through the mother's sacrifices.

Single mothers today are heading more households and the numbers continue to rise due to divorce, economics, crime, AIDS and other social issues that we face today. We want to celebrate what women have done for their sons. Some issues mother's face cross-cultural lines and some issues are specific to the African-American community. All mothers want the best for their sons. Every mother wants her son to grow up in a world that will embrace him educationally, socially and spiritually. It does not always happen that way.

For all of the mothers, grandmothers, aunts and stand-in mothers, through your sacrifice and commitment towards nurturing your sons from dreaming to becoming the men that are written about in this book, thank you for your love, devotion and support.

Chapter 16
Road Maps

Road-Map

Whether you a single mother, a married mother, a mother with a partner or a grandmother raising a male, it is important that you take care of yourself. I have included a "road-map" to help you on your journey of developing a healthy relationship with your son. These questions and suggestions apply to all age groups, regardless of your marital status. Put a check next to the answer that applies:

Birth to 2 years of age:

1. How often do you read to your son?

_____ Daily   _____ 2+ times a week   _____ Once a week
_____ Seldom   _____ Never

Note: Mothers should read to their sons daily. Pick a quiet time, evening or morning. Read at the same time daily. By reading to your son when he is young, you will be creating a love of reading as well as a spirit of adventure. You will begin to see your son's creativity come to life as a result of you reading stories to him.

2. How often do you pray for and with your son?

_____ Daily   _____ 2+ times per week   _____ Seldom
_____ Never

Note: Mothers should pray for their sons daily. Set aside a time morning, noon or night to pray specifically for your son. Also set aside time to pray *with* your son. By praying with him, you will be helping him to develop a spiritual life. He will learn who God is and that in addition to an earthly father he has a Heavenly father that is watching over him also.

3. What support network do you have in place to assist with the development of your son?

_____ Father _____ Grandparents ____ Family
_____ Friends _____ No one ____ Church

Note: It is important that you establish a support network to help with the raising of your son. Make sure males are actively available and involved with your son. By establishing these relationships, you are not only helping your son to grow, but you are also creating some "downtime" for yourself. If you have no one in town, ask the school to help recommend groups, mentors, or activities that will provide support for you and your son.

4. What are some activities you do to reduce the stress in your life?

_____Go to the movies _____ Read a book _____Shopping
_____ Other outings ____ Nothing

Note: It is important that mothers find positive outlets to reduce the stress of raising a child, working, and life related issues. Otherwise, you could become bitter and short-tempered.

5. What fun activities do you do with your son?

_____ Movies – how often? _____ times a week
_____ Parks – how often? _____ times a week
_____Outings – how often? _____ times a week

Note: By spending one-on-one time with your son in a relaxed atmosphere you will bring joy and fulfillment to both of your lives.

Don't forget to tell and show your son that you love him (hugs and kisses).

From 2 to 12 years of age:

1. Do you know your son's friends and their parents?

Friend _____	Parent's Name _____	
Friend _____	Parent's Name _____	
Friend _____	Parent's Name _____	
Friend _____	Parent's Name _____	

Note: It is important that you know your son's friends and their parents. This knowledge is helpful while monitoring your son's attitudes and behaviors. Don't forget to tell and show your son that you love him.

2. What type of savings have you established for your son's college or secondary education?

_____ Savings Bonds   ____ Insurance
_____ Education Savings Plan ____ Bank Account
_____ Other

Note: By having a savings plan, it will allow your son the opportunity to pursue his educational goals.
Have your son put money in a "Pursuit of Your Dreams" fund.

3. What goals are you setting and encouraging your son to reach?

____ Educational   ____ Vocational Interests
____ Sports   ____ Performing Arts
____ Science   ____ Other ____ None

Note: Early identification of your son's interest allows you the ability to shape and support his goals. Set expectations for all areas of his life. Tell him that you love him and that you are willing to do whatever it takes to help him achieve his dreams.

4. What school involvement do you participate in with your son?

___ PTA   ____ Parent Conferences
___ School Volunteer   ____ Open House

Note: It is important that parents are involved in their son's school. The more involvement and support that you give will reinforce the fact that his education is extremely important to you. Continue reading to or have your son read to you. This will alert you to any problems he might be having in school. This is also the stage when many males start losing interest in reading. Your interest might just be what will keep your son on the reading track and interested in school.

5. What type of responsibilities are you giving your son?

___ Cleaning his room   ____ Cooking
___ Taking out the trash   ____ Washing the car
___ Washing his clothes   ____ Cut the grass
___ Saving Money   ____ Working

Note: The more responsibility your son assumes at home, the more prepared your son will be to accept and handle responsibility in the real world.

Don't forget to tell and show your son that you love him (hugs and kisses).

Young Adulthood – 13 to 18 years old: Mothers should continue to be involved in their son's life. Mothers still should have knowledge of her son's friends and parents. This is the stage where young men's identities begin to take shape.

1. What are you involved in at your son's school?

___ PTA   ___ Parent Conferences
___ School Volunteer   ___ Open House

Note: This is a crucial development period for your son. This is the age where many young men reach the fork in the road. Parents *must* stay involved at all times to keep your son on the right track.

2. Who are your son's friends and their parents?

Friend _____ Parent's Name _____
Friend _____ Parent's Name _____
Friend _____ Parent's Name _____
Friend _____ Parent's Name _____

Note: Continued parental involvement is still needed to ensure that your son does not get involved with the wrong crowd.

3. How are you supporting your son's dreams?

_____ Finding a mentor in your son's field of choice
_____ Supporting his interests
_____ Attending his functions or activities

Note: Supporting your son's interests will cause him not to feel alone and will enhance his chances for success. *Critique your son's performance, but do not criticize your son.*

3. What fun things do you and your son do together?

____ Movies   ____ School activities/events
____ Amusement parks ____ Dinner/outings
____ Community Service

Note: Mothers that have outings with their sons help to teach them how to treat other females that will come into their life. It also provides a time of fun and relaxation. This is a great time to talk about each other's lives and stay in tuned to what is going on with each other.

4. What support are you giving to your son's goals?

____ College Visits   ___Vocational School Visit
____ Establish Savings ___ Help with applications

Note: Every young man may not want to attend college. Your son may choose a vocational school, the military or some other career. Be supportive of whatever he decides. Conversations about drugs, birth control, sex, violence and finances are still needed during this timeframe.

5. What spiritual activities does your son participate in?

____ Church, how often _____
____ Bible study, how often _____
____ Sunday School, how often _____
____ Youth Conferences, how often _____
____ Church Functions, how often _____

Note: The earlier and more consistent spiritual involvement your son has the more morally and spiritually sound your son will become. "Train a child in the way he should go and when he is old he will not turn from it," (Proverbs 22:6 NIV).

6. What social topics do you discuss with your son?

___ Drugs   ___ Gangs   ___ Crime
___ Weapons ___ Birth Control   ___ Sex

Note: Discuss these topics openly and honestly with your son. Depending on the maturity level of your son, these discussions may need to start as early as 4-5 years old. Today, some kindergarten children bring weapons to school, make inappropriate sexual gestures to others, etc. Make sure to provide age appropriate information. Remember that your son will get distorted information from older boys, television and music regarding these topics. It is the parents' responsibility to cover these topics properly and as often as needed.

Don't forget to tell and show your son that you love him (hugs and kisses)

Manhood: Things mothers should do:

1. How often do you have contact with your son?

____ Daily   ____ 2+ times a week

____ Once a month   ____ Seldom

____ Never

Note: At this stage in his life, your son should have his own municipal address (live somewhere else). It is still very important that you have contact with your son at least weekly. Depending on where you live, this contact may be in person or on the telephone. Your son still wants to hear your voice or to see you.

2. How do you handle your son's disappointments now?

____ Supportive   ____ Criticize

Note: Be very careful not to criticize your son's choices (job, wife, car, etc.). If he does share any disappointments with you, do not tell him what he should have done, or "I told you so." He is a man and he must make his own mistakes. Be supportive or be quiet!

Finally, if your relationship with your son has been broken for whatever the reason, here are some suggestions on how to bring healing and restoration to the relationship:

1. Continue to pray for your son.
2. Review the issues or events that caused the breakdown of the relationship. If you honestly do not know what caused the split, ask your son and be prepared to *listen* to his explanation.
3. Seek to understand your son's point of view more than trying to make your son understand your side.
4. Accept responsibility for your part of the disagreement or breakdown in the relationship.
5. Tell or reinforce to your son that you love him and desire to be reconciled with him.
6. Ask for your son's forgiveness or accept his apology.

7. Accept the fact that your son is now a man and that his ideas and opinions may be different than yours. You will now have to accept him as an adult.

Don't forget to tell and show your son that you love him (hugs and kisses).

In closing, remember that life is too short to hold grudges, so let old things pass and choose to be reconciled with your son. While your position should have changed within his life, the love he has for you will never change.

Journey

"Life is a journey. The journey is composed of ups and downs, the good and the bad, the joys and pains. But it is not these things that make the journey. The true essence is the opportunity to take the trip."

---Don E. Miller, Author

from "Poetically Yours, For the Heart Speaks"

Additional copies of this book or the first book written by Don E. Miller, *"Poetically Yours, For the Heart Speaks", can* be ordered through his website:

www.youngboldunique.com.

OR

You can send a money order for $12.95 ($10.95 + $2.00 for shipping and handling) to:

Young, Bold, Unique
P. O. Box 360313
Decatur, GA 30036-0313

Don E. Miller is available to speak at your banquet, seminar, youth, teacher or parent workshops, university, company or any other event/venue. Please contact him at:

Young, Bold Unique
(770) 523-2627 (office)
(770) 323-9452 (fax)

Or you can send your inquiry via email to:

ybu00@hotmail.com.